All concrete left

Albert Török

Albert Török

For you

CONTENTS

*

1. We make the same turns.....pg.9
2. My song.....pg.11
3. Lighthouse.....pg.13
4. Humble.....pg.15
5. Symphony.....pg.16
6. Dreamer.....pg.19
7. Middle of night.....pg.21
8. Emotions echoed on water.....pg.22
9. Touch.....pg.25
10. We are tangled.....pg.27

**

11. You jump above silent fountain.....pg.30
12. Diving.....pg.33
13. Behind curtains.....pg.35
14. Cautious with your wings.....pg.36
15. I walk in your light.....pg.39
16. My adulthood shed.....pg.41
17. All concrete left.....pg.42
18. Fragrance.....pg.45
19. Our circle.....pg.47
20. Meet you in the dark.....pg.48

***

21. Your request of beauty.....pg.53
22. With eyes kept on ground.....pg.55
23. Vanishing distance.....pg.56
24. Warm rain.....pg.59
25. Confession.....pg.61
26. Sinking.....pg.62
27. Mood swings.....pg.65
28. Pillars of light.....pg.67
29. Your heat.....pg.68
30. Mind's crystal.....pg.71

****

31. Walk on my thoughts.....pg.74
32. Parallel paths.....pg.77
33. Footprints.....pg.79
34. Your hiding.....pg.80

All concrete left

*

Albert Török

We make the same turns

You are so close,
I breathe your air
and let your hair
rest on my shoulders.

We make the same turns
by mistake
to collide each other
with lightness.

Remember,
our beginning started
with accidents
caused by attraction.

Your home became mine
when our patience overflowed
the gap between us.

Now I smile
when I see you
lying on my bed
and laughing with your eyes.

Albert Török

My song

*I sing
and my voice
fills space.*

*People walk,
their heads guided by thoughts
numb
to my signals.*

*My song
goes through walls
and penetrates ocean
to stimulate whales
in sleep.*

*They relay my message
to your mind
by going around earth
countless times
to find you.*

Lighthouse

Grown up waves
soak sandy shore
underneath my cliff.

I feel safe
high above ocean's unbounded effort
to swallow
all the seagulls.

Algae bathe
with heads nodding
and feet rooted on seabed.

You bathe in sun
then keep his light
to become lighthouse
for lost mariners

and save me
from my thoughts' ocean
where storms of my emotions
threaten to sink my boat.

Humble

I become humble
when god's sweat showers
to wash pollution off
and keep bees flying.

I smell your perfume
fresh after rain
enter my organs of perception
and settle on my inner walls.

Your deposit in my lungs
grows into mountain of joy
in my heated soul
unaccustomed to you.

I have to fly without wings
to drink from your well
offered free
for the thirsty.

Symphony

My breath deepens into slow cycles,
gasps and sighs remind me
of my urgency for air
and wake me from enchantment.

I am motionless,
became pure ear
only to listen
your chant.

Your song tells your story
with tones developed by your mother
to shape you
into a woman.

Are you ready to hear my voice?

I see you move,
your unconscious steps
abolish the gaps

and we go
to join couples
in earth's symphony.

Dreamer

My trust gone
for days of self sustained compassion
when spices sprinkled by your eyes
healed my wounds.

They stayed from my youth
when my soul accepted
raw impressions
without filters

and my mind
fresh in my flesh
was too innocent
to understand abuse.

Parts of me still alive
search for a dreamer
to anchor me
in her world of beauty.

Albert Török

Middle of night

Middle of night falls
and houses sleep in deep silence,
only you come
with purpose.

Your flame keeps you fresh
and fast like a seagull
on your direct course
above the unconscious landscape.

Lights of your car
throw beams on my wall
and raccoons move with slow motion
to note invasion of their privacy.

Your race to see me tonight
made you weary,
I carry you in my arms
and see my warmth sit on your skin.

Emotions echoed on water

Your boat rings on waves in coming storm.
What are you doing there?

Are you ready to be on open ocean
with your heart nurtured in my lake?

Dimensions shift
when the garden plant
throws herself to sea
and fresh rain
doesn't reach her lips.

Winds give you thrust
with half flexed muscles,
your sails swell
in foreshadow
of a strong blow.

Is shore close
or you have to fly faster than your imagination
on fluid mountains?

I hide in your muscles,
in waves,
in shapeshifting clouds...

Don't be scared,
I share your fate,

I die when you die
or live
after the trial of emotions echo on water.

We'll walk together with fused hands
on the narrow path between cliffs and sea
to our home.

Albert Török

Touch

Storm's skeleton
touch the prairie
with gentle contact
of immense weight.

The clouds' bone-frame
dissolves in a blink into an arrow
forged by compassion
between sky and earth.

Fire bounce on starved grass
and sparks trembling through land
only to be calmed by shower.

Your kiss starts identical burn in my nerves
then I blush
and your care is unable
to extinguish my blaze.

We are tangled

Melodies stranded in my head
were unable to leave me behind
in this world of challenge.

My body absorbed the tunes
and moved on rhythm
with low tones of a male base.

Then you came
with your high pitch
flying in chaotic order
through empty places of my atoms
and moving me off center.

Now we are tangled,
our tied knots
captured
in the symphony
of you and me.

Albert Török

All concrete left

**

Albert Török

You jump above silent fountain

You jump above silent fountain
with light heart,
not expecting water to shoot
from earth's hall
and bathe you
in deep passages' treasure.

Deposits of past
settle on your cloth
to enhance your natural charm,
they crystallize your curves
into a monument.

Come, sit on my laps
and don't break the magic
by moving from flawless present
to incomplete future.

Albert Török

Diving

Children run to catch balls,
their smiles knock on my window
inviting and alluring
into a world of growing.

I throw you a dream
pulled from threads
of my puzzled mind
after you left my bed
to dress in sunlight.

Your eagerness
meets her match
when you sink
under my sheets.

You move toward me
with light dancing on your shoulders,
jumping from your lips
and diving from your eyes into mine.

Albert Török

Behind curtains

*Standing behind curtains
won't help revealing your want,
your hunger grows
with your years.*

*You became careless
in search for a man,
buses empty their load at your steps
and men enter other homes.*

*By leaving your doors unlocked
you invite thieves,
they'll run with your heart
to sail rough waters.*

*I entered your rooms yesterday
and didn't find you,
watch out,
you made me a thief
with your kindness.*

Albert Török

Cautious with your wings

You walk cautiously with your wings
hidden in your pockets,

reflections on your skin,
tattoos of life
turn into wrinkles
to cover more of your youth
every year.

Is your beauty lost
or only transformed
into ripe seeds
of growth?

You bow
to pick up your thoughts
dropped
behind you,

then you see birds open their wings
to fly up with your seeds
and break the straight line
of reason.

Every memory was a pearl
in your neckless
around life's ocean,
now they sail
above life.

I turn at the corner and see you
displaying the whole range of human race,
you crowd my vision's field
exposing my future in repeated perseverance.

Albert Török

I walk in your light

I walk in your light
and sense your presence,
even though
you are on the other side of globe.

Earth's lens
focuses your rays
when they pass through crystals
under her skin.

I didn't know
our home is a giant heart
swimming in void
and connecting us together.

Would we become aliens
of distant stars,
when we step on other planets?

My adulthood shed

A small rumble starts inside me
when your arrival is announced
through loudspeakers
at the airport.

Only a few days past
without your mind
wrapping around my body

and I feel exposed,
too open
outside your shielding words
of advise.

My adulthood shed,
years of mature thoughts
gone,

now I can see you again
as I saw you
at first,
standing there naked
without my mind
wrapping around your body.

All concrete left

Heavy rain descends
from collapsing clouds of overflown sky,
and cities
woven into earth's dress
submerge.

My window-screen tremble
under rapid nocks,
while raindrops wash yesterday's dust
back to soil.

I met you the other day
in forest' womb
close to that road
filled with water.

You held my hand
on dry land
and not letting me go
home.

Would you let me leave
in water-world
of dream?

All concrete left
this changing universe of love
where sums of feelings
resurface
as an island of hope.

Fragrance

I imagine you hold a rose
I gave you as our symbol
of friendship.

We agreed for every word
I speak from now
is courtship.

Your long dark hair
fly on soft air
and cover my eyes.

I smell your fragrance
reaching
for my singleminded love

and I am not denying
your power
in distinct moments.

Our circle

Can I be whole without you?

When you came in new shapes
to seduce my longing soul
and damp my hunger,
our circle closed.

Your disappearance
only for short
cause me to shed
my human part.

I roar
in midst of well behaving men
and seek refuge
behind your sweet cage
of innocence.

Albert Török

Meet you in the dark

*Your picture preserves
unchanging youth
in my room.*

*Memories of my past
wait
between sheets of time.*

*You'll be stranger when we meet
under neon lights of dreams
tomorrow*

*and say words
we were shy of yesterday
when we lived in denial.*

*Our talk uncovers
emotions
buried deep in us.*

*I lower myself
to mine more
and meet you in the dark.*

***

Albert Török

Your request of beauty

I look at your face
and see myself in your eyes
unaltered
since we met behind the orchard.

Time flows,
present doesn't erode
in passing moments

and I don't find
my wrinkled skin
in your mirror.

You keep me young,
my dying cells renew
in your wish for me to stay
and fulfill your request of beauty.

With eyes kept on ground

I am far from men made lights
deep in the night
and watch falling stars
die.

I wish to hold them up
on imaginary plate
before they enter
our sphere.

They would be the ones
to survive
earth's core
of hardened light.

I start walking
with eyes kept on ground,
and wonder if I'd look at you
would my love pierce through your body?

Vanishing distance

I am blinded by light
jumping from you,
then stepping on my cells.

My smallest units of life
become mirrors
of their own image,

they echo
three dimensional shapes
of themselves.

You are my idea
of perfect harmony
emanating from my source

and I am your reflection
built by identical cells
under your guidance.

When we meet,
our atoms rush
to fill space

unaware
of vanishing distance
between us.

Separation is gone,
our bodies warm,
we become two suns
in strong hold.

Warm rain

I become childish once more
and run under warm rain
on unstable bridge.

The river below
with crocodiles of muddy shallows
looks at me with hunger.

Warm drops of light cloud
rest on my shoulders
reminding me your tears of joy
in our moments.

Are you ready to continue our dream
of a perfect world
planted on ruins of past failures?

Confession

I am with you
and feel alone,
my soul's deep
is lost
behind your ears.

I know you listen
to my words,
I bathe you
in my thoughts,

they reach and soak
into your skin
filling your reservoir
to overflow with sudden speed.

Then I see
rest of my confession
wash over you
and scatter in air
on others.

Sinking

*I am grounded to earth's center
with flow passing through my spine
and entering soil's coarseness
with ease.*

*My inertia is not weakness,
but a drop
holding the texture of continuum
as one.*

*My strength of riding tides
is rooted in harmony
within a big wave
of travelers.*

The current in energy's ocean
takes me down
to deep blues of our planet's psyche

where humans
like sardines
rarely venture.

I sink,
my body turns
into elements,

I become endless
with no horizon
to limit my heart.

Mood swings

Still air above dunes
stops this hot landscape of desire
into motionless beauty
of sand-waves.

Only your footprints suggest
life's invasion
into valleys
beyond knowledge.

You are lost
and your mood swings
take you closer
to sun.

Are you ready
to go
and have your burial
in fire?

I follow your signs
left behind
by your boots of self-reflection
and carry water of life
on my back.

Pillars of light

Your smile melts
my unwanted resistance
under trees
in the fabric of shades.

I sit between pillars of light
and observe you being one of them,
a beam shoots from you
to turn my magic switch on.

Your eyes
bathe me with rays
entering my body with constant flow
from you.

I become loyal
to your mind
and follow bouncing thoughts
on your lips.

I let you rest,
my sheet becomes
a flying carpet
under us.

Your heat

*I sit on a bank
and feel warmth flow through my bones,
my body divides sun's current
to keep blooming flowers safe
behind me.*

*The heat is strong,
wings on flies burn
and bushes bend closer to birds
to savor their feathers' breeze.*

*My skin bathe in nature's fever
when asphalt melts under geese' steps.*

All this heat is minor
to fire radiating from you
and ready to burn the sun,

but I step before you
to drink up your glow
on your lips.

Be merciless my love,
I was already burning before I knew you,
your sparks
turn into offsprings
between us.

Albert Török

Mind's crystal

My mind's crystal
invades my eyes
with reality resting on my doorsteps.

I look at you
and see a shape bent through lenses
to fit my anticipation of ideal.

Would you be someone else
for a man
with different perception,

when your invisible cells to me
become building blocks
in his imagination?

You would, like an alien,
walk in alternate world
with your other past

and attract
your other kind
with passion.

Albert Török

****

Walk on my thoughts

My car is my sleeping bag
on long roads,
that bind this strange land
with protective net.

I follow the words left by ancestors
when they traveled at time's beginning
with songs dropping behind them
on virgin ground.

Their language stayed
in rocks
covering earth's surface
with armor.

I lie on their chants
grown into grass
after centuries of repetition
and think of you.

Will you walk on my thoughts
millennia from now
when my bones gone
and only a piece of my consciousness lingers
on a different kind of ground?

My idea of you
sprouts all over
woven into winds,

I trust your image
on this land
for safekeeping.

Parallel paths

My clothe wobble
when you blink at me
with startle
and pinch my arm.

My demonstration of tenderness
was translated as rude
by your mind
grown in another world.

Would be worth
to build a bridge
between our cultures
divided by an ocean of hope?

We are on two parallel paths
meeting on special moments
when our universes crash
with joy.

Footprints

Jump!
I wait with my hands up
to meet you below your window
and give you safe landing
into my world.

Are you as brave as a baby bird
at her first flight,
who is ready to die
in her eagerness to live?

I know
your love is stronger than locked doors
or emotional chains of custom
when I feel your soft load
settle in my grasp.

Our footprints
laid ahead in stones
awake
under our weight

and we follow the road
made
by our trust
in change.

Albert Török

Your hiding

I pick up your scent
by watching squirrels leap on trees,
their steering tails
adjust for winds.

Explosions in my head
betray your nearness
again and again
in my nerve endings.

I look around in haste
and see a piece of your clothe
emerge and vanish
behind maple's core.

Your pounding heart
pressed to trunk
vibrates the tree
and squirrels feet start tingling.

Your hiding shows more of you
than any public act
when sea of your reflections
invade my mind.

Pond's water gives me your taste,
swan's neck your flexibility,
buds on trees recall
continuous renewal of your skin,

birds' feathers imitate your touch
by caressing winds' back,
I close my eyes
and see your imprint on my eyelids.

Albert Török

meditationcrumbs@gmail.com

www.ingramcontent.com/pod-product-compliance
Lightning Source LLC
Chambersburg PA
CBHW071611170526
45166CB00003B/1054